TRADITIONAL CRAFTS

By Linda Hetzer

Photographs by Steven Mays

Raintree

Milwaukee • Toronto • Melbourne • London

PROJECT DESIGNS: Basketry, Candlemaking, Madeleine Appell
Bookbinding, Millicent Trikaminas

PRODUCTION: Designer, Deborah Bracken
Illustrators, Lynn Matus and Sally Shimizu
Text editor, Jill Munves

Library of Congress Number: 77-28740

1 2 3 4 5 6 7 8 9 0 82 81 80 79 78

Printed and bound in the United States of America.

Library of Congress Cataloging in Publication Data

Hetzer, Linda.
    Traditional crafts.

    SUMMARY: Instructions for a selection of projects
involving basketry, candlemaking, and bookbinding.
    1. Basket making — Juvenile literature.
2. Candlemaking — Juvenile literature. 3. Bookbinding
— Juvenile literature. [1. Handicraft] I. Mays,
Steven. II. Shimizu, Sally. III. Matus, Lynn.
IV. Ttile
TT879.B3H47 745.5   77-28740
ISBN 0-8172-1190-X

SYMBOLS

The symbols that appear near the title of each project tell several things at a glance: how difficult the project is, about how much time it takes to finish it, and the kind of materials you need to make it.

Complexity

 Easy

 Average

 Challenging

Time

 One hour

 One afternoon

 Several days

Materials

 Found objects (things you have around the house)

 Variety store items

 Special craft tools or materials

CONTENTS

BASKETRY

Baskets are woven much like cloth is woven, except that in basketry there is no need for a loom. You weave a flexible thread over upright spokes. Because they are fairly rigid, the spokes determine the shape of the basket.

Basketry was probably one of the first crafts ever practiced. In ancient times, baskets were made from any coarse, flexible fiber such as dried grasses, reeds, or branches. Today, many materials are used for making baskets, including yarn, cord, ribbon, and pipe cleaners.

Early baskets were made as useful objects. They were used for storing food and gathering fish. Canoe frames and even the walls of huts were actually large baskets made of woven grass and twigs. Nowadays, we use baskets for decoration or to hold small things such as bread, picnic foods, fruit, or yarn.

In the projects on the following pages, you will learn how to make baskets from empty margarine tubs, from corrugated cardboard, from ribbons and cardboard strips, and from clothesline cord.

MATERIALS

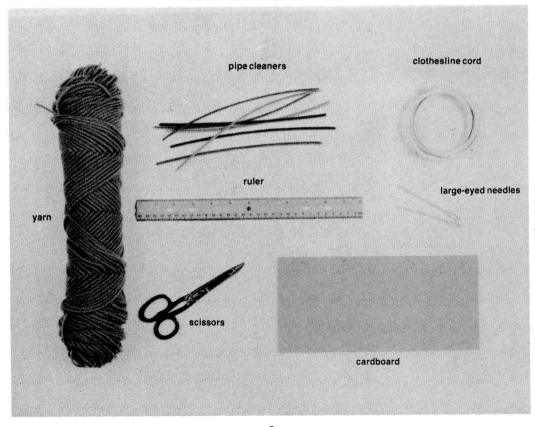

pipe cleaners

clothesline cord

ruler

large-eyed needles

yarn

scissors

cardboard

Tub basket

One way to learn how to make a basket is to start with a shape—in this case, a plastic margarine tub—and to weave on it. The type of basket weaving used in this project is known as twining. In addition to the plastic tub, you will need scissors, pencil, ruler, a large-eyed plastic needle, and assorted leftover yarns.

2 Cut a slit from the rim of the tub all the way down the side at each of the marks. These 1-in. (2.5-cm) pieces are the spokes you will weave on.

1 Measure, and mark 1-in. (2.5-cm) intervals around the top of the plastic tub.

3 Cut a 2-yd. (1.82-m)-long piece of yarn, and fold it in half. Slip the loop over any spoke in the plastic tub, positioning it so half the yarn is behind it.

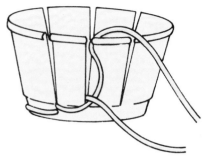

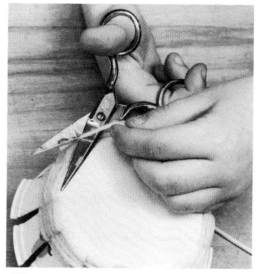

4 To twine, cross the back yarn over the front yarn. Bring the back yarn in front of the next spoke and bring the front yarn behind the next spoke. Continue twisting the yarn in this fashion to weave around the spokes.

7 Trim the yarn ends at the bottom of the tub on both the inside and the outside so the basket will be neat.

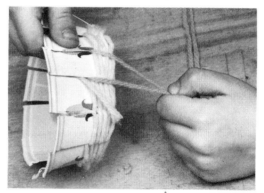

5 When you run out of yarn or want to change colors, fold a new piece of yarn in half and slip the loop over the next spoke to be woven.

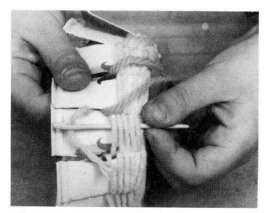

6 Thread the yarn end that is on the outside of the tub through a large-eyed needle. Slip the yarn end under the weaving on the front, bringing it down to the bottom of the tub. Repeat this with the yarn end inside the tub.

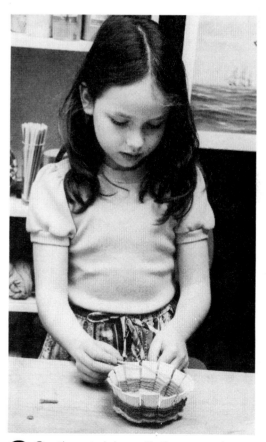

8 Continue twining with the new color. You can change colors as many times as you want. At the top of the basket, hide the yarn ends in the weaving the same way you did for changing colors.

These colorful twined baskets were once plain plastic margarine tubs. The tubs were transformed into baskets with pieces of leftover yarn.

Twined basket

Twining is a versatile type of basket weaving because it can be used with so many different kinds of materials. To make the twined basket on the following page, you will need a 1½-x-12-in. (3.8-x-30.4-cm) piece of corrugated cardboard, eight 12-in. (30.4-cm)-long pipe cleaners, a large-eyed plastic needle, scissors, masking tape, and a few ounces (grams) of rug yarn.

1 Fold the cardboard strip in half and open it up again.

2 Fold the strip in quarters by bringing each end in to the fold in the center. Open up the cardboard.

4 Corrugated cardboard has spaces in the center layer. To make the spokes for the basket, put pipe cleaners through the spaces. Starting at one corner, count down three spaces and put the pipe cleaner in the fourth space. Push the pipe cleaner only halfway through.

3 Make a square with the cardboard. Each fold will be a corner. At the fourth corner, tape the two ends together with masking tape.

5 Bend the pipe cleaner, count three spaces, and put the free end of the pipe cleaner in the fourth space. Adjust the ends of the pipe cleaner to make them even; then push the looped end flat against the cardboard so the spokes are as long as possible. Repeat this around the cardboard square, always leaving three spaces between pipe cleaners. You should end up with two pipe cleaners—or four spokes—on each side of the square.

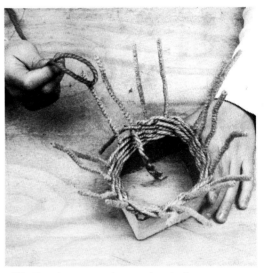

6 Push pipe cleaners so they slant from the center of the box. The basket should be wider at the top than at the base. Cut a 2-yd. (1.82-m) length of yarn, fold it in half, and slip the loop over any spoke.

8 To change colors or to start a new piece of yarn, cut a 2-yd. (1.82-m) length of yarn. Fold it in half and slip it over the spoke next to the one you are ending the old yarn on.

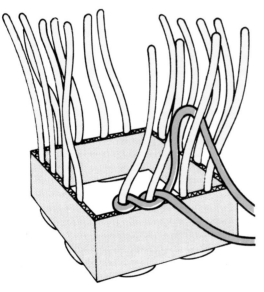

7 To twine, cross the back yarn over the front yarn and bring the front yarn behind the next pipe cleaner. Continue around the basket, crossing the yarn in the corner spaces also. The basket will become round as you weave. The tighter you pull the yarn, the straighter your basket will be. The looser you weave, the wider it will be.

9 To hide the yarn ends, thread each one through a large-eyed needle and bring it down through the weaving, next to the spoke. Trim off the excess. Continue twining with the new color. Work until there is only 1 in. (2.5 cm) of pipe cleaner exposed.

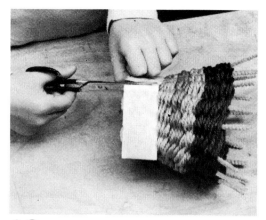

10 To form the bottom of the basket, cut the cardboard at each of the four corners.

11 Holding onto the basket firmly, fold each piece of cardboard flat in turn. Tuck one end of the last flap under the first flap, as shown.

12 To finish the top edge of the basket, fold each pipe cleaner to form a loop. Tuck the end in the same space the spoke is in.

A basket made of cardboard, rug yarn, and pipe cleaners is an ideal holder for a dried-flower arrangement.

Ribbon basket

You can make a pretty basket out of strips of cardboard and pieces of grosgrain ribbon. You will need a 9-x-12-in. (22.8-x-30.4-cm) piece of cardboard, scissors, white glue, masking tape, ruler, and 18-in. (45.7-cm) lengths of grosgrain ribbon in assorted widths. The number of ribbons you will need depends on the width of each ribbon. If you use 1-in. (2.5-cm)-wide ribbons, you will need four 18-in. (45.7-cm) lengths.

1 On a 12-in. (30.4-cm) piece of card-board, mark 1-in. (2.5-cm) intervals across both short sides. Draw lines down the length of the cardboard, connecting the marks. Cut out the cardboard strips along the lines you have drawn. You will need nine strips.

2 Put four strips in front of you, placing them about ⅛ in. (.31 cm) apart. Put a piece of masking tape across one end to keep the strips in place.

3 To make the base of the basket, weave four strips across the center of the strips that are taped to the table. Take the first extra strip and weave it under the first taped strip, over the next, under the next, and over the last one. Weave the second strip in the opposite way, going over the first taped strip, under the second, over the third, and under the fourth. Weave the third strip the same as the first and the fourth strip the same as the second.

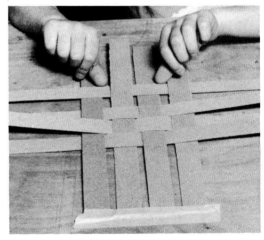

4 When you have finished weaving, push the four strips close together to form a tight weave. Make sure the woven area is in the center of the strips from top to bottom and from left to right.

10

5 To form the sides of the basket, lightly score the cardboard strips so you can fold them up without breaking them. To do this, place a ruler across the strips at the edge of the woven area. Use the point of your scissors to make a line on the cardboard strips. Score them on all four sides.

7 Just above the bottom of the basket, glue the end of a ribbon to the inside of one strip.

8 Weave the ribbon over the next strip and under the next. Continuing to weave over and under, go around the entire basket.

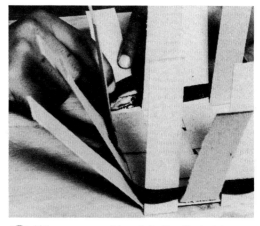

6 Remove the masking tape and gently fold up each strip on the scored line.

9 When you get back to the first strip, tighten the ribbon until the strips stand up. Glue the end on top of the beginning end and cut off the excess.

10 Glue the next ribbon just above the first ribbon on the same cardboard strip you ended on.

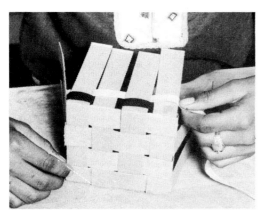

11 Weave this ribbon in the opposite way from the first. Go under the strips you went over before and over the strips you went under. When you reach the first strip, glue the end in place. Continue weaving this way until you are almost at the top of the cardboard strips.

12 Trim the cardboard along the top if it is uneven.

13 To make a handle, put glue on the last cardboard strip and cover it with a piece of ribbon.

14 Curve the handle and glue the ends to the inside of the basket. Hold the ends in place for a few minutes while the glue dries.

These colorful ribbon-and-cardboard baskets can be used as Easter baskets, party favors, or just to brighten up a room.

Coiled basket

Coiling is a technique for making baskets in which you use two different cords: a pretty one that will show and a strong one for the foundation. For the baskets on the following page, we used clothesline cord for the foundation and rug yarn for the decorative wrapping. The exact amount you need will depend on the size basket you make. But 2-yd. (1.82-m) lengths of both clothesline cord and yarn are good amounts to start with. You will also need a large-eyed metal needle, glue, masking tape, and scissors.

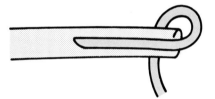

1 Thread one end of the yarn through the needle. Overlap the other end with the clothesline cord for about 1 in. (2.5 cm). Wrap the yarn around the cord, starting at the end of the cord and covering the yarn end as you wrap (bottom).

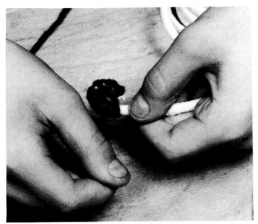

2 Fold the wrapped end of the cord around itself and wrap yarn around both pieces of cord to keep the bend secure.

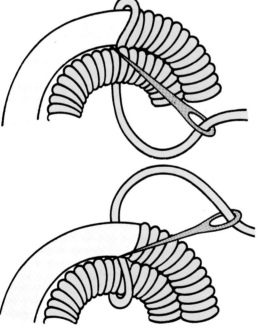

3 The first loop is the beginning of the coiled bottom of the basket. Continue to wrap the cord with yarn and coil it tightly around the first loop. Every five or six wraps, secure the cord you are covering to the cord inside it with a figure-eight stitch. To do this, bring the yarn around the inside cord and put the needle in the space between the cords (top). Then bring the yarn around the outermost cord and put the needle in the space between the cords again (bottom).

4 Continue until the bottom is as large as you want. Then begin building up the sides of the basket by coiling the clothesline cord on top of itself. Wrap the yarn around the cord several times. Secure the new round with the figure-eight stitch.

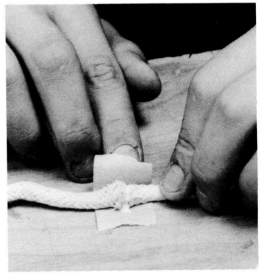

5 If you want to add more cord, put glue on the ends of the old and new pieces and place them together. Wrap a piece of masking tape around the joining. (When you wrap the yarn around the cord, it will cover the tape.)

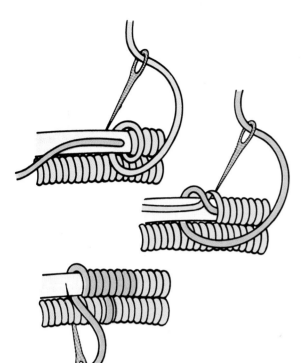

8 Make several figure-eight stitches to secure the end of the cord to the round below it. Then bring the needle under the last few wraps and cut off the excess yarn.

6 To change colors or to start a new piece of yarn, lay the end of the new yarn on the cord before you finish with the old yarn (top). Continue wrapping with the old yarn until you have secured the new end. Then thread the needle with the new yarn and lay the end of the old yarn on the cord (center). Continue wrapping and stitching with the new yarn. This will secure the end of the old yarn under the wrapping (bottom).

Using the technique of wrapping and coiling, Bryan made a large green and purple basket with a matching cover. Gabrielle made a small brown and orange basket.

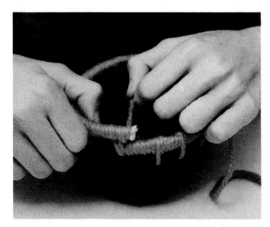

7 To finish the basket, cut the cord where you want it to end. Put glue on it, and wrap the yarn around the cord, right up to the end.

15

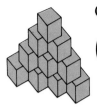

Openwork basket

The wrapping-and-coiling technique used in the previous projects can also be worked into open, airy designs. To make one, you will need clothesline cord, rug yarn, a large-eyed needle, and scissors.

2 Continue wrapping and stitching. The cords will touch one another only where you secure them with a figure-eight stitch. You can shape the spaces somewhat by deciding where to put these stitches.

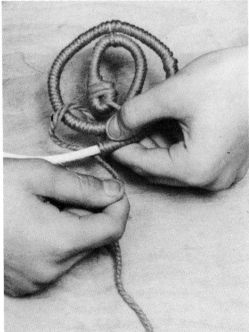

1 Begin the wrapping and coiling as described for the coiled basket. But instead of placing each coil right next to the previous one, leave some open spaces. To do this, wrap several inches (cm) of the cord. Then use the figure-eight stitch to secure sections of the cord where you want them to meet.

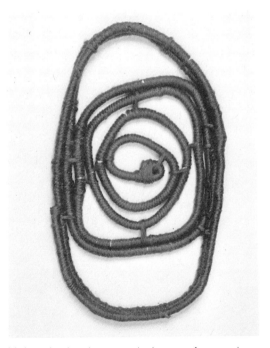

Using the basketry techniques of wrapping and coiling, Bryan has made an open-work design that can be used to hold large objects — or be mounted on a wall for everyone to admire.

CANDLE MAKING

Years ago, people read, dressed, and cooked by candlelight. Today, since we have light at the flick of a switch, we use candles only for decoration. The projects that follow will show you how to make six types.

When you make candles, always have an adult with you. Cover your work area with newspaper, and have all your supplies ready before you start to melt the wax.

For the wax, you will need paraffin (available at the grocery store) and pieces of crayon, which add color to the wax. Hot wax can catch on fire, so it should never be melted directly over a flame. The photograph on the opposite page shows you how to melt wax safely. Put three or four pieces of paraffin and crayon in empty metal cans. Set them in a large pot of water, and clip them to the pot with clothespins. Put the pot of water on a stove or hot plate. Turn the heat on; the water will boil and the wax will melt. To use the melted wax, remove the clothespin and hold the can with a pot holder.

Candlemaking can be fun when it is done properly and safely. And it is nice to have light provided by candles you have made yourself.

MATERIALS

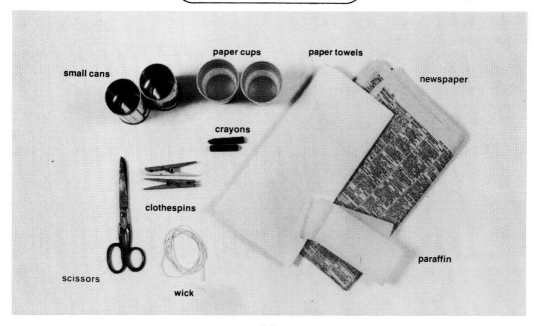

small cans   paper cups   paper towels   newspaper   crayons   clothespins   scissors   wick   paraffin

Molded candles

Many kinds of containers can be used to make molded candles. Using disposable molds, such as wax-paper cups and juice containers, makes it easy to remove the finished candle from the mold. You simply tear the mold away. That's how the candles shown here were made.

In addition to the molds and the materials for melting the wax (see introduction), you will need wicking (available at hobby stores), scissors, pencils, masking tape, pot holders, a bowl full of ice, paraffin, and crayons. If you want to make striped candles like the ones shown on the next page, you'll need crayons in several colors.

1 Crayons provide the color for the candles. Peel the paper wrappers from the crayons, and break the crayons into 1-in. (2.5-cm) pieces.

19

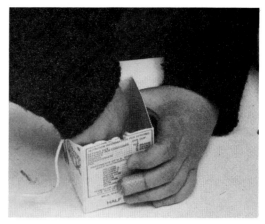

4 Put a piece of masking tape on the end of the wick. Tape it to the bottom of the mold, placing it in the center.

2 Melt the paraffin as described in the introduction. Then gently drop several pieces of crayon into each can. (Use only one color for each can.) As the crayons melt, gently stir them with a stick or the end of a paintbrush. Melt as many colors of wax as you want to use in your candle. When the wax has melted, turn the heat off.

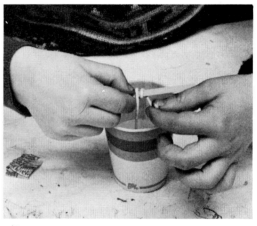

5 Roll the top end of the wick around a holder, like a pencil or a dowel, and rest the holder on top of the mold.

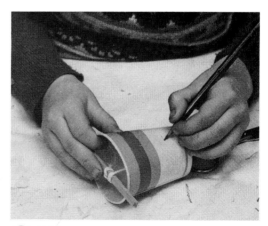

3 To prepare the mold for the wax, cut a piece of wick that is 3 in. (7.6 cm) longer than the mold is tall.

6 With a pencil, mark the side of the mold, dividing it into as many stripes as you want in your candle.

9 Choose the color wax for the second stripe, and pour it into the mold up to the second mark. Put the mold into the bowl of ice to harden the wax. Repeat these procedures to make the rest of the stripes.

7 Once you have the mold prepared, you are ready to make the candle itself. Using a pot holder to protect your hand, take a can of melted wax from the pot. Pour wax into the mold, up to the first mark you made. This will be the first stripe. If you are going to use that color again, put the can of wax back into the pot of water.

10 When the last layer of wax has hardened, peel the paper cup or juice container from the candle.

8 Put the mold into a bowl of ice and hold it there for a few minutes. The ice will harden the wax. Each layer must be hard before you pour in the next; otherwise, the colors will mix. When you see the wax begin to harden, take the mold out of the bowl of ice.

11 With scissors, cut the wick so only ½ in. (1.2 cm) sticks out from the top of the finished candle.

21

Dana gazes into the candlelight provided by four striped candles, molded in paper cups and juice containers.

Dipped candles

A dipped candle—made by dipping a piece of wick into melted wax over and over again—is one of the easiest, and probably one of the oldest, types of candles you can make.

To make a dipped candle, melt the wax as described in the introduction, and gather your other materials: a wick and a bucket or jar full of cold water.

1 Cut a piece of wick twice as long as you want your candle to be. 12 in. (30.4 cm) is a good length. Dip the bottom half of the wick into a can of melted wax.

2 As soon as you have dipped the wick in the wax, dip it into the bucket of cold water. The cold water will set the wax, making it cool enough to touch. Straighten the wick with your hand. (It has a tendency to curl and bend.)

3 Continue dipping, first into the wax and then into the water. If you skip the water, the hot wax will melt the layer before it, and the layers will not build up. As the layers of wax build up, the candle will get straighter and straighter.

4 You can dip into wax of different colors. Just remember to dip the candle into cold water first. As the wax drips down, it forms the tapered shape. The bottom of the candle will be much wider than the top.

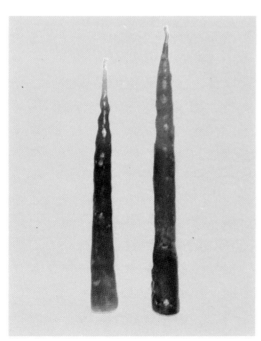

5 When the candle is about 1 in. (2.5 cm) in diameter, dip it into the cold water for the last time. Roll it on a piece of paper to get an evenly rounded surface. Cut the wick at the top of the candle to a length of approximately ½ in. (1.2 cm).

Ice-cube candles

Ice cubes and melted wax don't mix. As you've seen in earlier projects, ice hardens wax and keeps it from flowing. Mixing ice cubes and melted wax, you can create a candle with unexpected holes and crevices.

You will need melted wax (see introduction), a 1-qt. (1-liter) milk carton cut to be 6 in. (15.2 cm) high, a 4- or 5-in. (10.1- or 12.7-cm) candle that is ½ in. (1.2 cm) thick, and a bucket of ice cubes.

These hand-dipped candles were made from many layers of wax. When the candles are lit, the melting wax will form a rainbow of colors.

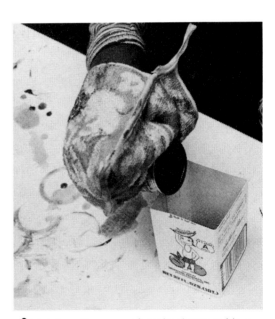

1 Holding the can of melted wax with a potholder, pour a ½-in. (1.2-cm) layer of wax on the bottom of the shortened milk container.

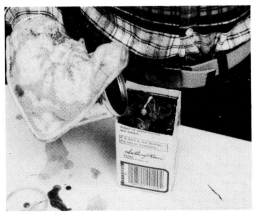

4 Using a pot holder to protect your hand, pour melted wax into the container – all the way to the top of the candle. Set the container aside for about an hour, until the ice cubes melt.

2 Put the candle in the center of the milk container. The wax in the bottom will help hold the candle in place.

5 When the ice has melted, pour out the water.

3 Carefully put ice cubes all around the candle. Make sure it remains upright and in the center of the container.

6 To unmold the candle, gently tear the milk carton away from it.

These candles look like ancient rock formations full of crevices and caves. But years of rain and wind were not needed to form them. They were created in a few minutes with ice and melted wax.

Sand-cast candles

Candle molds are usually ready-made containers like juice cans or milk cartons. But you can also create a mold by digging a shape in damp sand.

   To make sand-cast candles, you will need melted wax (see introduction), wick, a bucket of damp sand, and shells or rope for decoration.

1 Trace the shape candle you want on the sand. Following the outline, dig out enough sand to make a mold or container for the wax. You can make the candle as big or little as you want, but it's good to make it at least half as deep as it is wide.

2 To add decoration to the candle, you can use shells or rope in the mold. If you use shells, press the outside of each one into the sand, as that is the side that will show on the finished candle.

4 Cut a piece of wick twice as long as the mold is deep. Place one end of the wick on the sand at the bottom of the mold, right in the center. Wrap the other end around a pencil, and rest the pencil on the top of the sand.

3 If you want to make a rope hanger for the candle, lay two pieces of strong rope or cord in your sand mold. Cross them in the center, and make sure the ends stick out beyond the mold. Later, when the candle has set, you can tie the four ends together and hang the candle from a hook. (Do not light this candle; use it only for decoration.)

5 Holding the can of melted wax with a pot holder, pour wax into the sand mold. Fill it so the wax is level with the top of the sand. Let the candle harden overnight. Remove it from the sand and trim the wick.

Sand-cast candles can remind you of a favorite trip to the ocean. A thin layer of the sand used for the mold sticks to the candles; the shells add extra decoration.

Ice-cream candles

Would you like to have an ice-cream soda sitting on your table all the time? You can if it is a candle. To make this candle, you will need melted wax, a glass, an ice-cream scoop, a plastic fork, and a straw, in addition to the tools described earlier.

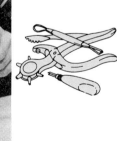

1 Cut a piece of wick 3 in. (7.6 cm) longer than the height of your glass. Tape one end to the bottom of the glass with masking tape. Wrap the other end around a pencil and rest the pencil on top of the glass. Put a straw in the glass.

28

2 The ingredients of an ice-cream soda are syrup, soda, ice-cream, whipped cream, and a cherry. To make the syrup, pour a small amount of melted wax into the bottom of the glass. Tilt the glass so the wax runs up one side. Do this in several places, and it will look like syrup dripped down the glass.

4 To make ice cream, pour some wax into a milk or juice container. Hold the container in a bowl of ice while you whip it with a plastic fork.

3 Choose the flavor soda you want and pour melted wax (in the appropriate color) into the glass, stopping about 1 in. (2.5 cm) from the top.

5 Cut the wick so it is 2 in. (5 cm) higher than the glass. Fill an ice-cream scoop with the whipped wax, while it is still soft, and place the wax on the soda. Be careful not to cover the wick.

6 For the whipped cream, whip some plain melted paraffin, and spoon it on top of the ice cream.

7 To make a cherry, take a small piece of red wax that has cooled, and roll it into a ball. Place it on top of the ice cream.

These ice-cream sodas look good enough to eat. Only the wick sticking out of the top lets you know they're not.

Rolled candles

The rolled-and-carved candles shown on the opposite page started out as flat slabs of wax made on cookie sheets. In the photographs that follow, you will see how they were transformed into candles.

To make these candles you need melted wax in several colors, one cookie sheet for each color, vegetable shortening, wax paper, a plastic knife, and a 4-in. (10.1-cm) long candle in any color you like.

2 Let the wax set for 10 to 15 minutes. It will be solid but not completely hard. With a plastic knife, cut the wax into 4-in. (10.1-cm)-wide slabs.

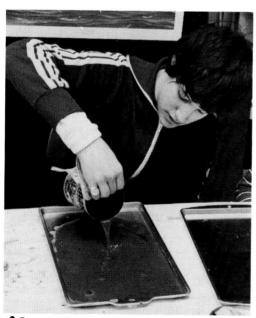

1 Grease the cookie sheets by covering them with a thin layer of shortening. This keeps the wax from sticking to the metal. Pour enough wax onto each sheet to make a 1-in. (2.5-cm)-thick slab. Use a different color for each cookie sheet.

3 Carefully lift the wax slabs from the cookie sheets, and put them on a piece of wax paper.

4 Take one slab of each color you use, and lay the slabs on top of each other. Start each piece 2 in. (2.5 cm) down from the last so that at each end, the stack of slabs is only 1 in. (2.5 cm) thick.

7 When you have finished the carving, turn the candle on its side. Trim the bottom flat, so the candle won't wobble.

5 Place the candle on the beginning end, aligning it at the edge so the wick sticks out. Roll the wax slabs around the candle. Where the slabs end, each color of wax will show.

The carved designs of these rolled candles reveal the various colors of wax used to make them. By using layers of wax in different colors and carving it in various places, you can create candles as intricate and varied as these.

6 To make the candles even more colorful, use the plastic knife to carve a design in the wax. This will expose the different colors in the layers below.

BOOK BINDING

You read books at school and you take books out of the library, but did you ever think about making a book? You can make your own books for your stories, poems, drawings, vacation pictures, or anything else you can think of.

There are two different ways to bind books. The pages are either glued or sewn into the cover. Sewn bindings are strong so they are used in books that get a lot of use like library books. Glued bindings are more common. They are found in both the hardcover and the paperback books that you buy in a bookstore. You can make books with both glued and sewn bindings.

In the projects on the following pages, you will learn how to make a sewn book with colorful pages and an accordion book that folds up to a small size but opens up to be very large. You can also make a book that stays together without any glue, a photograph album with black pages, a cloth-covered diary, and a portfolio for your drawings.

You can make a book and write a story in it. Then let your friends come over to borrow it, just like they do from a library.

MATERIALS

ribbon

cloth tape

cardboard

construction paper

typing paper

cloth

glue

scissors

Sewn book

You can make your own book and fill it with pages of all colors. You need a 10-x-16-in. (25.4-x-40.6-cm) piece of lightweight cardboard, a 12-x-18-in. (30.4-x-45.7-cm) sheet of construction paper for the cover, a 9-x-15-in. (22.8-x-38.1-cm) sheet for the inside cover, and six 9½-x-15-in. (24.1-x-38.1-cm) sheets for the pages. You also need cloth tape, scissors, ruler, white glue, sewing needle and thread, rubber cement, watercolors, and paintbrushes.

2 Fold the cardboard along the line, being careful not to break it. Open it up again.

3 Place the cardboard, with the fold facing down, on top of the 12-x-18-in. (30.4-x-45.7-cm) construction paper. Center it and fold the excess paper over on all sides. Glue the overlap to the cardboard.

1 Begin by folding the cover in half. Hold a ruler in the center of the cardboard—8 in. (20.3 cm) from either side. Open the scissors and run one point down the cardboard, leaning it against the ruler.

4 Put glue on one side of the 9-x-15-in. (22.8-x-38.1-cm) construction paper. Center it on top of the cardboard so it covers the cardboard and the edges of the overlapped construction paper.

5 To make the pages, align the six pieces of construction paper so the edges are even. Fold them in half.

6 Place the pages on top of the cardboard cover, aligning the folds in both. Thread the needle with a long thread, knotting the two ends together so the thread is doubled. At one end of the cover, bring the needle up through the cover and out through the pages. Always point the needle away from yourself.

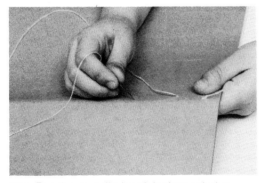

7 Put the needle back in through the pages and bring it out through the cardboard. Continue making long straight stitches along the fold. At the end, knot the thread on the outside.

8 To cover the stitching and to reinforce the spine, put a piece of cloth tape along the fold on the outside of the book.

9 For decoration, draw a design on the cover with rubber cement. Let it dry for a few minutes.

36

Both of these brightly covered books have pages of many colors also. The pages are sewn to the covers to make sturdy books.

10 Paint over the entire cover. The paint will not stick to the paper where there is rubber cement. Those areas will stay the color of the construction paper.

11 When the paint has dried, take off the rubber cement by rubbing your finger against it.

Accordion book

You can make a book that is only 4-x-6-in. (10.1-x-15.2-cm) when it is closed, but opens up to almost 2 yds. (1.82 m) long. You will need two 4-x-6-in. (10.1-x-15.2-cm) pieces of cardboard, an 18-x-24-in. (45.7-x-60.9-cm) piece of unlined white paper (available at art stores), tempera paint, paintbrushes, shellac, clear tape, scissors, white glue, a ruler, and magazine pictures.

1 Paint one side of both pieces of cardboard. Let the paint dry.

2 When the paint is dry, apply shellac with a paintbrush. The shellac protects the covers and makes them shiny.

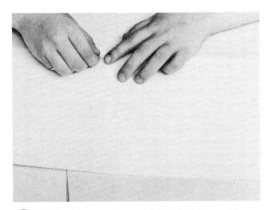

3 With ruler and pencil, divide the white paper into thirds so you have three pieces that measure 6 x 24 in. (15.2 x 60.9 cm). Cut them out, then lay the strips together with the short ends touching. Tape the pieces together to make one strip that is 6 x 72 in. (15.2 x 188.8 cm).

4 Measure 4 in. (10.1 cm) in from one end of the strip and draw a line. Fold the paper along that line.

5 Turn the paper over, measure another 4 in. (10.1 cm), and fold the paper again. Continue folding 4-in. (10.1-cm) sections, turning the paper over each time. This is accordion-folding.

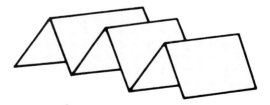

6 When you finish the folding, the paper will look like this, but it will be much longer and have more folds in it.

38

7 Glue the last rectangle on one end of the paper to the back of one cardboard cover. At the other end, glue the last rectangle to the back of the other cardboard cover.

8 You can decorate the front cover of the book, as well as the inside pages, by gluing magazine pictures to them.

Dana looks through the book she made with animal pictures. When she closes the book, it will be as small as the book lying in front of hers.

No-glue book

Can you make a book without using glue on the cover? Impossible? Not really. To make this book, all you need to know is how to fold paper. You need two 6-x-9-in. (15.2-x-22.8-cm) pieces of cardboard, two 9-x-12-in. (22.8-x-30.4-cm) pieces and two 6-x-18-in. (15.2-x-45.7-cm) pieces of construction paper for the covers, one 9-x-3-in. (22.8-x-7.6-cm) piece of construction paper for the spine, 12 pieces of typing paper for the pages, scissors, ruler, needle and thread.

2 The overlapped paper will meet and form a seam on the cardboard. Turn the cardboard over so the seam is face-down. Place it on top of a 9-x-12-in. (22.8-30.4-cm) piece of paper, aligning the 9-in. (22.8-cm) sides. Fold over the excess paper along the top and bottom edges.

1 Use one piece of cardboard for the front cover and one for the back cover. Make the covers separately and put them together later. To begin the front cover, place the cardboard in the middle of one 6-x-18-in. (15.2-x-45.7-cm) piece of paper. Fold over the excess paper on the two sides.

3 Remove this second piece of paper, and slip the folded flaps between the cardboard and the first piece of paper. You have now covered a piece of cardboard with construction paper without using any glue. Repeat this procedure to make the back cover.

4 To make the pages, fold the 12 pieces of typing paper in half. Thread a needle and knot the two thread ends. Stitch the pages together along the fold, leaving both the beginning and ending knots on the outside.

6 For the spine, fold the 9-x-3-in. (22.8-7.6-cm) piece of construction paper in half lengthwise. Then slip it through the front and back covers so it covers the stitching on the pages.

5 To attach the covers to the book, slip the first and last pages between the cardboard and the construction paper.

7 If you want to decorate the cover, cut out geometric shapes from construction paper. Glue these shapes to the front cover. This is the only time you need to use glue in the entire book.

It's almost like magic to make a book by simply folding paper, but these books are held together without glue.

Photograph album

To make a photograph album you need a 10-x-12½-in. (25.4-x-31.7-cm) piece of sturdy cardboard, a 10-x-14½-in. (25.4-x-36.8-cm) piece of construction paper for the spine and underneath covers, two 9-x-12½-in. (22.8-x-31.7-cm) pieces of construction paper for top covers, six 9-x-12-in. (22.8-x-30.4-cm) pieces of black paper for the pages, cloth tape, double-faced tape, scissors, ruler, and white glue. To decorate the cover with your initials, you need an alphabet stencil (available at variety stores) and felt-tipped markers.

1 Find the middle of the short side of the cardboard and draw a line down from the center. Then draw a line on both sides of the center line, ⅛ in. (.31 cm) away from it. These two lines—which are ¼ in. (.63 cm) apart—form the spine.

2 Score the two outside lines so you can fold them. Place a ruler along each line and run the point of the scissors along the line. Do not score the center line.

3 Form the spine by folding the cardboard along both scored lines. Reinforce it with a piece of cloth tape.

4 Place the cardboard, taped side down, on the 10-x-14½-in. (25.4-x-36.8-cm) construction paper. Fold the excess paper over top and bottom edges and glue it in place.

5 Turn the cardboard cover over. Place the two 9-12½-in. (22.8-x-31.7-cm) pieces of paper over the front and back covers, leaving the spine exposed. Glue these papers in place. There will be a large overlap on both covers. Don't cut it away.

6 Turn the cover over. Fold the excess cover paper over on both sides and glue it to the inside covers.

43

7 Cut a 12½-in. (31.7-cm) piece of double-faced tape, and peel off the protective paper on one side. Place tape on spine on the inside of the album. Then peel off the top layer of protective paper.

8 Fold the six pieces of black paper in half lengthwise. Put the pages into the album one by one, pressing the fold of each page against the tape.

9 Protect the edges of the album with cloth tape. Cut a piece to the length of each of the six edges. Put half the tape on the front of the cover, and fold the other half over to the inside.

10 You can decorate the cover with your initials. Place an alphabet stencil on the cover, positioning it so your letter is where you want it. Fill in the letter with a felt-tipped marker.

Jaime glued photograph corners (available at variety stores) on the pages of his photograph album. That way, he can change pictures whenever new favorites come along.

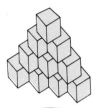

Diary

A diary is one of the most special books you can own, since it is a book about you. And a diary you make is even more special. To make a cloth-covered one, you will need two 6-x-9-in. (15.2-x-22.8-cm) pieces of cardboard, an 11-x-15-in. (27.9-x-38.1-cm) piece of cloth, 12 sheets of typing paper, scissors, white glue, needle, and thread.

2 Place the cloth face-down. Adjust it so the longer edge is horizontal with the edge of the table. Place the two pieces of cardboard, glued side down, on the cloth. Allow ¼ in. (.63 cm) between the pieces and about 1 in. (2.5 cm) of cloth all around the edges.

1 Put glue on both pieces of cardboard, and spread it into an even layer with a piece of paper.

3 Put glue along the six outside edges of the cardboard, and fold the excess cloth over on the two long sides.

4 Put a lot of glue on the corners. Tuck the excess cloth in, as shown; then fold the short side over the cardboard.

5 To make the pages, fold the 12 pieces of typing paper in half. Stitch the pages along the fold, following the directions given for the no-glue book.

6 Place the pages on top of the cover, with the stitching lying in the space between the pieces of cardboard. Glue the first page to the inside front cover and the last page to the inside back cover.

A personal diary can be covered with an interesting cloth cover—and then be filled with interesting things about you.

Portfolio

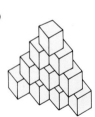

A portfolio is a flexible case with a hinged cover. The portfolio in this project is held together with three ribbon ties—one on top and one on each side. To make a portfolio, you will need one 20-x-30-in. (50.8-x-76.2-cm) illustration board, a 24-x-34-in. (60.9-x-86.3-cm) piece of vinyl (a plastic cloth available at variety stores), a 19-x-29-in. (48.2-x-73.6-cm) piece of vinyl to line the inside of the case, cloth tape; 1 yd. (91.4 cm) of ribbon, a long ruler, scissors, and a pencil.

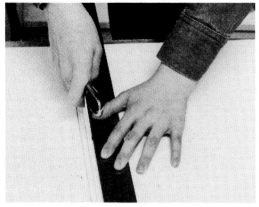

1 Find the center of the illustration board—15 in. (38.1 cm) in from either side. Draw a line. Then draw a line on either side of the center line, ¼ in. (.63 cm) from it. Score two outside lines with the scissor's tip, using the ruler as a guide.

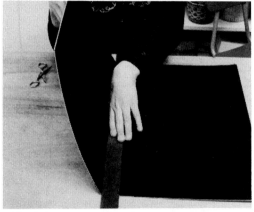

2 Fold the board on the two scored lines by holding the ruler against the line and gently folding the board.

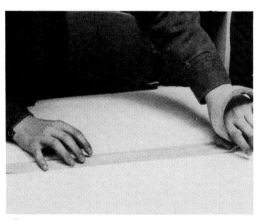

3 Reinforce the folds by putting a piece of cloth tape along the spine.

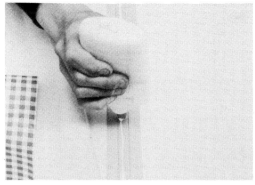

4 Put glue along the cloth tape on the spine. Put the large sheet of vinyl on top of the board, centering it, and press down on the spine. (You don't have to glue the entire board, only the spine.)

5 Turn the board over. Fold the excess vinyl over the short sides and glue it in place. Put a piece of masking tape on it to hold it until the glue dries. On the two long sides, cut a slit in the excess vinyl at the spine. Fold the ends under at an angle. Glue the long sides to the cardboard.

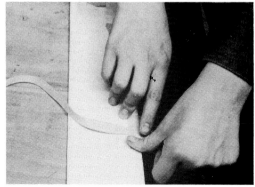

6 Cut six 6-in. (15.2-cm) pieces of ribbon. With cloth tape, put one piece of ribbon in the center of the top, bottom, and side of each piece.

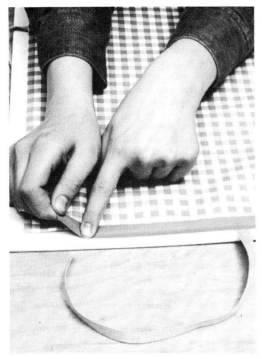

7 Center the piece of vinyl for the lining on top of the board, with the ribbon ties away from the center. Put cloth tape on all four edges of the lining.

8 You can decorate the front of your portfolio with pieces of cloth tape in any design you choose.

Lauren is showing some drawings to Leo (left) and Bryan (right) who are carrying their portfolios comfortably under their arms.